W9-APS-313

NATIVE NATIONS OF NORTH AMERICA

LIFE IN A
LONGHOUSE VILLAGE

LAZARE/PARKER

Bobbie Kalman

 Crabtree Publishing Company

www.crabtreebooks.com

LIFE IN A
LONGHOUSE VILLAGE

Created by Bobbie Kalman

(Dedicated by Barbara Bedell)
For my Mother

Author and Editor-in-Chief
Bobbie Kalman

Researcher and editor
Deanna Brady

Copy editors
Niki Walker
Amanda Bishop

Photo research
Jaimie Nathan

Computer and Graphic design
Kymberley McKee Murphy

Production coordinator
Heather Fitzpatrick

Consultants
Jackie Labonte, Literacy Coordinator,
  Niagara Regional Native Centre
Deanna Brady, Corporate Board Director,
  PHO 2000 American Indian Outreach Programs;
  American Indian Changing Spirits
Professor J.S. Milloy, The Frost Centre for Canadian
  and Native Studies, Trent University

Special thanks to:
Lewis and Eleanor Parker for being
  gracious hosts
Marc Crabtree for photographing much
  of the artwork

Photographs and reproductions
© Permission of Lewis Parker: cover, pages 4,
  5 (bottom), 6, 22 (top), 25 (top), 29 (top), 30
© Permission of Lazare & Parker: back cover,
  pages 1, 8-9, 10 (center), 11, 14 (top), 16, 17,
  18, 21 (bottom), 26, 27 (top), 28, 29 (bottom)
Sainte Marie among the Hurons: pages 19 (top),
  21 (top)

Illustrations
Barbara Bedell: page 5 (top), 7 (top), 10 (bear),
  12 (bottom), 13, 15 (right), 19, 20, 22 (left),
  23, 24, 25 (bottom), 26 (bottom), 27 (bottom)
Margaret Amy Reiach: pages 10 (wolf, beaver,
  turtle), 12 (top and center), 14 (bottom),
  23 (racks), back-cover hide
Bonna Rouse: page 7, 15 (left), 16 (bottom),
  interior backgrounds 1-3, 31, 32

Crabtree Publishing Company

www.crabtreebooks.com   1-800-387-7650

PMB 16A	612 Welland Ave.	73 Lime Walk
350 Fifth Ave.	St. Catharines	Headington
Suite 3308	Ontario	Oxford
New York, NY	Canada	OX3 7AD
10118	L2M 5V6	United Kingdom

Copyright © **2001 CRABTREE PUBLISHING COMPANY**. All
rights reserved. No part of this publication may be reproduced,
stored in a retrieval system or be transmitted in any form or by
any means, electronic, mechanical, photocopying, recording, or
otherwise, without the prior written permission of Crabtree
Publishing Company.

Cataloging in Publication Data
Kalman, Bobbie
  Life in a longhouse village / Bobbie Kalman.
    p. cm. -- (Native nations of North America)
  Includes index.
  ISBN 0-7787-0370-3 (RLB) -- ISBN 0-7787-0462-9 (pbk.)
  This book introduces children to the traditional daily life
of the Native nations who lived in longhouses and shared a
common way of life.
  1. Iroquois Indians--Juvenile literature. 2. Longhouses--
Juvenile literature. [Iroquois Indians. 2. Indians of North
America--Northeastern States. 3. Longhouses. 4 Dwellings.]
I. Title. II. Series.
E99.I7 K26 2001
974.7′0049755--dc21
                                    LC00-069364
                                    CIP

CONTENTS

The people who lived in longhouses

The **indigenous**, or Native, people who lived in the northeastern woodlands of North America built **lodges**, or homes, called **longhouses**. A longhouse is a large rectangular wooden building that is longer than it is wide. Its width and height are the same.

Iroquoian speakers

The languages spoken by most longhouse dwellers belonged to the Iroquoian language group. Many Iroquoian speakers lived in the southeastern area of North America. Some migrated north to settle in what is now New York State. Others settled in the provinces of Ontario and Quebec. In those days, the United States and Canada did not yet exist.

Breaking into bands

Before they migrated, the Iroquoian peoples were one **nation**. When they moved to the Northeast, different **bands**, or groups of families, settled in different areas. They grew in number and became separate nations, each with its own language and culture.

Who were the Iroquois?

The name "Iroquois" is a French name given to a league of five Iroquoian-speaking nations, who called themselves **Haudenosaunee**. They were also known as People of the Longhouse, but they were not the only people who lived in longhouses. The Iroquoian-speaking nations of the northeastern woodlands who were not part of the league, such as the Wendat and Erie, also lived in longhouses.

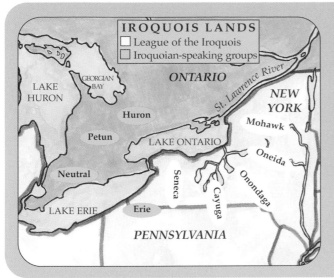

IROQUOIS LANDS
☐ League of the Iroquois
☐ Iroquoian-speaking groups

The Five Nations who called themselves Haudenosaunee were the Mohawk, Oneida, Onondaga, Cayuga, and Seneca. They settled along the southern shores of Lake Ontario and in the Finger Lakes area of New York State. The Huron, or Wendat, settled along Georgian Bay. The Petun, or Tobacco, lived southeast of the Wendat, and the Erie, on the southern shores of Lake Erie. The Neutral lived near Niagara Falls. The Tuscarora, Wenrohronon, Meherrin, Susquehannock, Nottoway, and Cherokee, also spoke Iroquoian languages, but these nations did not live in the Northeast. The Tuscarora, however, later moved north.

The Five Nations, which formed the League of the Iroquois, lived in territories that lay side by side. The League imagined this row of nations as a longhouse with five fireplaces under one great roof, as the man in the picture is shown drawing. The Mohawk were the Keepers of the Eastern Door, and the Seneca were the Keepers of the Western Door. The Onondaga, in the center, were the Fire Keepers because the council meetings were held in their territory. The Five Nations became Six Nations when the Tuscarora joined them about two hundred years later.

A longhouse village

Longhouse villages were built along the shores of rivers and streams so people would have a fresh supply of water for drinking and bathing. A waterway nearby also allowed the villagers to travel easily by boat. A village site contained many longhouses, which were arranged in a random pattern to prevent the spread of fires. There were also other common structures in the village, such as ceremonial lodges and medicine and storage huts. Some villages were home to as many as two thousand people! The size of a village depended greatly on how much wild food was available in that area.

Building a longhouse

Before building a longhouse, men went into the forest to find young elm, cedar, or birch trees. They peeled the bark from the trees, dried it, and cut it into large sheets. They made long wooden poles from the thin tree trunks. On a clear, flat area of ground, the men traced the shape of the longhouse in the soil and dug deep holes into which the poles would be placed. To make the framework,

Bark sheets were strapped onto the frame using bark strips.

the builders set the poles into the ground about three feet apart. The tops of the long poles were bent toward the center and strapped together with bark strips. The roof was curved or peaked so that snow would slide off and not cause it to collapse.

The frame

To complete the frame, **saplings**, or young trees, were wrapped sideways across the poles for support. Beams or rafters were tied under the roof inside to brace the structure. The men then covered the walls and roof with bark sheets, rough side out, which they tied on with bark strips. For extra protection, they set more upright poles on the outside of the bark to hold it firmly in place. There was a door made of bark or animal hides at one or both ends of the longhouse. The low doorway kept in the heat.

*Longhouse villages were encircled by **palisades**, or walls of heavy poles sharpened to points at the top. To prevent sneak attacks, there was only one entrance. Outside the palisades were cornfields. Villagers moved every ten to fifteen years, when the soil around the village was no longer fertile enough for growing crops.*

Sharing one room

Inside, a longhouse was one big room, which was sectioned off from one end to the other and divided by a central corridor. Individual families lived in each section, on either side of the corridor, and each section had a fireplace, which was shared by the families on both sides. The fireplaces were dug into the corridor floor, and there were holes in the roof above them to allow smoke to escape.

Single-family compartments

On either side of the fireplaces, wide sleeping bunks were attached to the walls, with storage shelves above them. The bunks formed single family compartments, which were separated from one another by woven screens. Families could hang mats or hides in front of their bunks for added privacy, but many left them open to take advantage of the heat from the fireplaces.

Hanging from the rafters

Food was stored in different ways inside the longhouse. Some foods were hung from the rafters or storage racks. Cornhusks were braided together, and strings of corn were hung to dry with squashes and other foods.

Storage pits

Many longhouses also had storage pits dug into the earthen floors. These were lined with bark and filled with dried corn, meat, or valuables. Water was kept in pottery jars that were made and decorated by the women. Families stored possessions on shelves, under their beds, or in boxes buried in shallow pits.

Staying indoors

In winter, villagers spent much of their time indoors. The men and older boys were sometimes away on hunting trips. The women, children, and grandparents stayed indoors, huddled around the warm fires.

Smoke-filled lodges

When it rained or snowed, the smoke holes of the longhouse were closed. During those times, the longhouses filled with smoke. Many longhouse dwellers suffered from lung and eye damage.

In this Wendat longhouse, two mothers are preparing food with the help of their young daughters. A baby hangs in a cradleboard, watching the activities taking place around her. Above the woman to her right, a hide is being stretched on a wooden frame. The people on the opposite page are placing a bucket of corn into a storage pit to keep mice and other pests from eating this food.

Family and village structures

Each longhouse was the home of a **clan**, which was made up of 15 to 20 families. Sometimes a clan occupied several longhouses. Members of a family included parents and children, but a clan also included aunts, uncles, nieces, nephews, and cousins. A clan traced its descent back through its mothers, grandmothers, and great-grandmothers to a female **ancestor**. The head of the clan was the **matron**, or clan mother. The men of a clan hunted together, and the women helped one another with planting and cooking. The longhouse and fields belonged to the women of the clan, and the weapons and tools belonged to the men.

The clan's emblem

Over the doorway of each longhouse was the **emblem**, or symbol, of the clan who lived inside. The emblem stood for the animal that was believed to be the clan's guardian, and the clan was named after that animal. Examples of clan symbols are wolf, beaver, bear, and turtle. Each clan had stories about how it was named after that animal.

Part of a huge family

People of the same clan often lived in different villages and belonged to different nations, but they were always welcomed when they visited one another's lodges. If people from the Turtle Clan, for example, visited another village, they stayed in the longhouse of the Turtle Clan of that village.

The number of clans that lived in a longhouse village or were part of a nation varied. Some nations had only three or four clans, but some, such as the Wendat, had eight. A clan relationship was considered a family relationship, and its members were not allowed to marry one another.

Marriage and children

Marriages were arranged by mothers. A young man's mother picked out a wife for her son and then talked to the girl's mother, who had the right to refuse the offer if the young man was not a skilled hunter or warrior. The clan mother, however, had the final say about the marriage. Without her approval, the wedding could not take place. When a suitable match was made, the husband came to live in the wife's longhouse but spent much of his time in the longhouse of his own clan. Any children born to the couple were considered part of the wife's clan, and she gave them their names.

The sachems

With the help of the other women, the clan matron selected the **sachem**, or chief, who represented her clan in the **village council**. There were two kinds of sachems—**civil** and **war** sachems. There was also a head sachem for the whole village. Village council meetings were held at the longhouse of the head sachem. The war sachems met in a secret location.

Council meetings

The village council discussed matters such as hunting, fishing, ceremonies, and the building of longhouses. It also helped resolve disputes and put into practice the wishes of the villagers. The **tribal council** included the sachems from several villages of one or more nations. It decided on issues such as trade and war among nations.

(right) People took turns speaking on issues. This sachem is giving his opinions on a village matter. To make a decision on a village or tribal matter, all the sachems had to agree and vote unanimously.

(above) This young woman was chosen to be the wife of this young man. They exchange gifts, and he will move into her clan's longhouse.

Food from the land

To feed their families, the people of the longhouse village hunted animals, gathered plant foods, and planted several kinds of crops. The men were in charge of hunting, fishing, and trapping. They tracked, killed, and brought back to the villages deer, elk, moose, bear, and beaver. The men trapped birds such as geese, ducks, and pigeons in large nets hung between trees. They thanked the animals they hunted for sacrificing their lives to feed people.

Helping one another

Sometimes large groups of men went hunting together. They cooperated in driving groups of animals into a river or an enclosure they built. This herding method was also used in fishing with traps. Sometimes the men took their families or clans along on longer hunting or gathering trips. They set up camp and lived away from the village until there

was enough food to take home. Each family member worked hard to preserve the meat, fish, or seafood that they would take back to the village. They dried and smoked the meat on racks that hung above a fire.

A bounty of foods

Women gathered many kinds of foods that grew wild in the woods and meadows around their villages. The villagers ate seeds and nuts out of the shell or cooked and mashed them with powdered meat. They used milkweed, mustard greens, dandelions, and skunk cabbage in salads or stews. They added mushrooms to soups or boiled and fried them as a side dish. Wild fruits were eaten fresh, made into sauces, or dried for later use. Apples were baked in hot ashes. Dried cherries were added to soups. Some fruits and herbs were made into juices or teas.

A sweet time!

In the early spring, the maple trees thawed and began to release their sap. The sap could be boiled to make syrup for sweetening food. At the first sign of warm weather, the villagers went on camping trips to the maple groves to make enough maple syrup to last all year. Children looked forward to this special time because they received sweet treats of maple sugar. After the trees were tapped, the sap was boiled until it became syrup. The mothers ladled some of the hot syrup into molds laid on top of the snow. It hardened and turned into maple sugar. The children couldn't wait to sample this tasty treat!

Growing corn, beans, and squash

The longhouse villagers found much of their food in nature, but they also grew crops such as sunflowers and melons. The basic crops they grew—corn, beans, and squash— were known as the "Three Sisters." The name "Sisters" also refers to the spirits of these plants. The women planted the three vegetables together in rows so the bean stalks would wind around the corn stalks for support. Squashes grew between these stalks to shade the ground, keep it moist, and stop weeds from growing.

The most important Sister

Of the Three Sisters, corn was the most important. Each nation had **societies**, or clubs, of women who took care of the planting each year, after the men cleared the fields. A planting ceremony was held, and then women and girls headed out to the fields with their aprons filled with corn kernels and their voices raised in song. They planted the kernels in mounds to protect them from the cold. They planted two rows in every field and later went back to finish each one. By planting two rows at a time, no one felt that her field was being planted last. This method of planting also ensured that some corn would be ready for harvest after the first crop of corn had been eaten.

Different kinds of corn

Different kinds of corn were used for different purposes. One was a starchy type known as **bread corn**, which was dried and stored for later use. To prepare it, the women boiled the dried corn kernels in water, to which they added wood ashes to help loosen the **hulls**, or outer skins.

Making cornmeal

When the corn had dried again, it was put into a **mortar** and pounded into **cornmeal** using a **pestle**. Sometimes two women, or a mother and daughter, pounded together. The women sifted the cornmeal through loosely woven baskets into trays made of bark and used the trays to mix the fine cornmeal into dough for bread or corn cakes.

Mush and popcorn

Flint corn was dried and stored for use all year. Before cooking, it was crushed and then boiled until it became a soft mush. Dried fish, meat, or oil were added for flavor. Popping corn was popped by being shaken over hot coals.

Corn on the cob

Green corn was actually a tender, milky white corn that was cooked on the cob. It was a favorite dish when it was freshly harvested. It could also be stored after it had been charred in the fire. Before the ears of green corn were roasted, the cornhusks were loosened and pulled back, and the cornsilk was removed. The husks were then slid back into place, and the ears were buried in ashes and covered with hot coals until they were cooked.

The mortar was made from a hollowed-out tree stump or log, and the pestle was carved from maple wood. It was narrower in the middle to make it easy to hold.

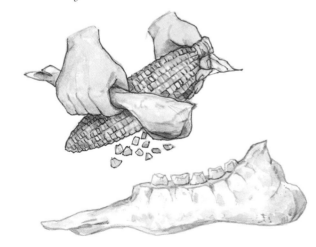

Dried corn kernels were scraped off the cobs using a deer jaw. They were stored in a basket made of bark.

Preparing and cooking food

Women prepared and cooked all the meals. They rose early to begin shelling corn and pounding it into meal for making bread. The pounding woke everyone in the village, letting them know that breakfast was being made. The women mixed the cornmeal with cooked black beans and made large, thick pancakes, which they boiled and served with pine-needle tea sweetened with maple sugar.

Meals were cooked in clay pots, which were hung over the fire. Dinner was started early and simmered all day, so those who were hungry could eat anytime. This meal was often a stew consisting of meat or corn and beans. Both green and dried beans made a delicious soup or stew, with deer or bear meat added for flavor.

Food and hospitality

Women made sure that there was always food cooking for their husbands and relatives as well as for visitors. When guests came to call, the women offered them something to eat.

It was considered polite for visitors to eat what was offered. Visitors stayed as long as they wished and were sometimes even adopted into the families they visited.

What a feast!

For special occasions, such as the wedding shown in this picture, a feast was held. Some foods were cooked in the longhouse, and other dishes were baked in a **trench oven** outdoors.

A large pit was dug into the ground, and rocks were heated inside it over a wood fire. Various kinds of foods were baked in this trench oven, including several vegetables and eggs in their shells. They were baked one on top of another.

The different foods were separated by layers of coals or ashes and covered with moist sand or earth. **Venison**, or deer meat, was roasted on a pole over a large bonfire.

The jobs of family members

Men and women had different jobs in the longhouse village, although they helped one another with many tasks. Men built the longhouses, palisades, and canoes, traded with other nations, and were in charge of hunting and fishing. They cleared land for farming by **girdling** the trees, setting fire to their bases, and cutting down the trunks with stone axes.

Protecting their families

The men defended and protected the women, children, and older people of the village. They were expected to be fearless at all times and to ignore pain, hunger, and cold. Men were trained from birth to be brave.

They learned to fight at a very young age and were ready to fend off an animal attack or a raid by another nation. Men also conducted raids on enemy nations. Often, one or more nations raided the village of an enemy nation and took prisoners. Iroquoian men were proud of being great warriors!

The men did the trading

Various northeastern nations traded with one another and with nations farther south and west. They traded for things that were scarce in one region but found more easily in others. Some Iroquoian-speaking nations traded with the eastern Algonkian-speaking nations.

The Wendat were the most successful traders because they remained friendly with their Algonkian neighbors. They traded for fur pelts, birchbark canoes, and warm clothing. The Wendat and Haudenosaunee did not trade directly, but they did get one another's goods through trade with other nations.

Women's work

Women were the heart and soul of the longhouse village. They had many jobs in and outside the longhouse. They gathered wild foods from the land, planted corn and other vegetables, and raised the children. Women also prepared the hides from which clothing was made, sewed the clothing, made pottery, and wove baskets and mats from cornhusks, wood strips, and grasses. From bark, women made trays, boxes, and sturdy barrels for storing dried foods. They fashioned pots and bowls from soft clay. They decorated the pots by scraping designs into the clay.

The elders

The **elders** of the longhouse were grandparents or older uncles and aunts who were respected advisers in the village. They played a very important role in teaching the children the skills they needed in life. From the time children could walk, the elders taught them how to behave and do all the things they needed to do to become responsible and successful adults.

Learning the history

Before the Europeans came, nothing was written down. Family, clan, and tribal histories were taught through stories. Grandmothers and grandfathers and other storytellers told stories of how their people lived in days gone by. They also recounted events in history and told legends about animals that gave examples of the "right" ways to behave in daily life. The stories were told carefully and passed down from generation to generation.

Children and adults alike loved to hear stories told by elders.

Children's lives

Native children led very busy lives, but they also had plenty of time to play and have fun. Children were loved and honored because they represented the future of the nations. They were almost always included in family and clan activities.

Strong and brave

It was very important for children to make their families proud and avoid cause for shame. Children learned how to be strong and brave by watching the behavior of the adults and older children. They learned how to be honorable and considerate members of their families, clans, and nations.

No complaining

Except in cases of emergency, children were discouraged from complaining about pain or discomfort, just as the adults around them did not show such weakness. From birth, many children were bathed every day in the cold waters of the rivers or lakes near their homes. Some were taken into lodges filled with hot steam. They learned not to mind heat or cold.

Silence is golden!

Babies were encouraged not to cry, and children were taught to walk silently. These lessons were important in avoiding attacks by wild animals or enemies. Children learned how to ignore hardships in their surroundings or circumstances.

A school without walls

Iroquoian children did not go to school. They learned everything by watching and listening. Girls watched the women of the village as they worked together. They were encouraged to learn each task by imitating the women. They also copied the behavior of the older females and followed their advice. Girls prepared meals for special occasions and made beautiful gifts such as baskets and moccasins for their brothers and other relatives and friends. They helped with planting, making clothes, and fashioning pots and baskets from clay and bark.

Lessons for boys

Fathers, grandfathers, uncles, and cousins taught boys how to run quickly and how to make tools and weapons. The boys learned by helping the men hunt, fish, paddle canoes, and defend their families. At an early age, each boy was expected to go into the woods alone and track his first game animal. Although he might have to drag a deer by its antlers most of the way home, when he reached the edge of the village, he would try to carry it over his shoulders to show his strength.

Passage into adulthood

When boys became young men, they went into the forest alone to seek spiritual wisdom, which might be revealed as a dream or vision. While alone, a boy did not eat for a week or more and prayed that a guardian spirit, such as a porcupine, would appear to him and tell him about his future. The spirit might give him a message and a song that would protect him whenever he was in danger or afraid.

Materials from nature

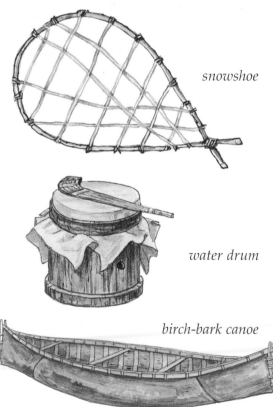

snowshoe

water drum

birch-bark canoe

(above) *The Iroquois made some canoes with bark stripped from tree trunks.*

Everything people wore and used was made from natural things they found in their environment. Tools used in hunting, fishing, and trading were made from wood, stone, shells, horns, and other parts of animals such as teeth and bones. No part of an animal was wasted! Bows and arrows, clubs, hatchets, spears, and knives were also fashioned from the same materials. Snowshoes were made from leather strips and wood and canoes from bark or carved tree trunks.

Tough rawhide

After the men hunted animals and brought them back to the camps or villages, the women were in charge of preparing the **hides**, or skins, which were used to make many items. Preparing hides involved several steps and took many hours of hard work. If the hide was left to dry, it became tough. This tough hide, known as **rawhide**, was used to make drumheads and other objects that needed to be hard and durable.

Preserving hides

Clothing was made from the hides of animals such as deer, elk, or moose. Before the hides could be used as leather material for clothing, they had to be preserved by a method known as **tanning** to keep them from spoiling or rotting. Tanning also made the hides soft.

Several ways to tan a hide

Tanning could be accomplished in a few ways. One way was to soak the hide in a solution made from the bark, acorns, and leaves of oak trees or other plants. This solution contained **tannic acid**, from which the term "tanning" comes. Depending on the plant that was used, the finished leather became tinted in various shades of tan. Some people soaked the hide in the animal's urine or rubbed its oily brains and liver into the hide to soften it. After being rubbed, the hides were stretched and dried. They were then smoked over a wood fire so they would repel bugs and remain soft after getting wet.

Women skinned the animals using a piece of sharp rock or shell. They tied the hides on wooden racks or hung them over logs and scraped off any meat, fat, or gristle that remained on the inside of the hides.

The hides were soaked until they were clean. After soaking, they were stretched and put onto racks to dry.

Clothing and regalia

Before the 1600s, the clothing of longhouse dwellers was made of animal hide or fur, sewn together with **sinew**. The clothes were decorated with flattened porcupine quills, moose hair, natural paints, shells, and bone.

Men's and boys' clothes

The basic clothing of men consisted of a **breechcloth** and **moccasins**. A breechcloth is a long strip of soft deer hide. It is wrapped between the legs, then up and under a belt or sash, with the edges hanging over the belt in the front and back. Moccasins are soft hide shoes. Shoes were also made from woven cornhusks.

Neither men nor women wore shirts or tops in warm weather. In cooler weather, men wore a hide shirt, **leggings**, and a **kilt**, or short skirt. Leggings were like tubular pant legs attached with loops to a belt and wrapped with decorated garters below the knee.

Women and children

The clothing of women and girls was not very different from that worn by men. In warm weather, women wore only a leather skirt and moccasins made of cornhusk or hide. Young children wore little or no clothing. When it was cooler, they added skin tunics or jackets, leggings, and robes made of animal fur.

robe

breech-cloth

garter

leggings

Furs came from beavers, bobcats, squirrels, raccoons, and wolves. Both men and women wore moccasins.

Regalia

Men and women wore and carried special accessories known as **regalia**. Regalia consisted of belts, headgear, bags, and tools. In the early days, these objects were made of wood, shells, feathers, horns, bone, and other natural materials. People made them for themselves or received them as gifts for performing good deeds. Belts were made from snake skin or were hand woven from natural fibers and strung with rows of shell beads.

*Men often **tweezed**, or pulled out, sections of their hair with clamshells. They also singed the hair or shaved areas with flint stones, leaving only a topknot or single row. This hairstyle became known as a "Mohawk." Women wore their hair long and loose or tied it at the back of the neck. Men and women sometimes decorated their face and body with **hapes**, or symbols, that had important meanings for them.*

hapes

Mohawk hairstyle

gustoweh

*Men sometimes wore a headdress called a **gustoweh**, which had a different design for each nation. The number and position of the feathers indicated the nation to which the wearer belonged.*

Many opportunities for fun

People of the longhouse enjoyed life. They held many celebrations throughout the year, but they also took pleasure in simple daily activities. There was always a lot of action inside the crowded longhouse. People told stories, played games, enjoyed one another's company, and were just happy to be alive! They especially enjoyed music and dancing. Their songs and dances were accompanied by the rhythm of rattles made of turtle shells and wooden drums filled with water. The dancers moved counter-clockwise in a circle, stomping their feet to the beat.

Women and girls enjoyed playing games in which they hid shells or pieces of bone under moccasins or mats while others guessed where the objects were hidden.

In the Bean Game, shown above left, women painted beans white on one side and black on the other. They competed to see who could strike the bowl against the ground and make five beans turn either black or white side up. The women below them are examining **wampum**, or "strings of white beads." Wampum, or "memory" belts were used to keep records.

Playing lacrosse

Lacrosse was one of the favorite sports of children and adults alike. It was played between opposing teams using a deerskin ball stuffed with fur and a long wooden stick with a small net at one end. Clans often played in small games, but sometimes the games were huge, with hundreds of people playing at once. Teams of several nations competed against one another. The games went on into the night, accompanied by singing and drumming.

Outdoor fun for children

Girls made work fun. They went as a group to fetch water, gather reeds and rushes, and pick wild berries. They played throwing and tossing games, using objects such as fruit pits. The games played by boys strengthened their bodies and improved their skills as hunters and warriors. Boys held races and competitions in wrestling, throwing hatchets, spearing fish, and shooting arrows. In winter, children made bark toboggans and raced them down nearby hills.

The Iroquois had a passion for lacrosse. Some games were played on enormous fields with thousands of players. Lacrosse became Canada's national sport.

Snowsnake

Snowsnake was a favorite winter sport. The object of the game was to throw a **snowsnake**, which was a long, narrow pole, down a trench dug into the snow. Each person tried to get his or her snowsnake to slide the farthest, while others tried to disrupt his concentration with cheers and yells.

Beliefs, ceremony, and celebrations

The Green Corn Ceremony, held in August, lasted several days and nights. The celebration featured songs and dances to "Our Mother" (Earth), who gave people this important food.

Many celebrations and thanks-giving ceremonies were held to show gratitude for the natural blessings that were a part of life. People gave thanks for the beginning of each new year, the time when the maple sap began to flow, the planting and harvesting of the crops, and the ripening of corn, beans, and strawberries, which they celebrated with festivals. They gave thanks for their ancestors, for all living creatures, for the earth, sun, moon, stars, wind, thunder, water, trees, and fire. They taught their children to greet each new day with a prayer of thanks.

Grateful to nature

Native people cared about their environment, especially because they depended on it so much. They were careful not to use up the natural resources such as the animals, plants, and soil. They planned their lives around the cycles of the seasons.

Mindful of other creatures

Hunters asked silent permission from the animals they killed and thanked them for providing food and clothing for the families of the hunters. They hunted in different places so they would not kill too many animals in any area. They did not hunt female animals before they had their babies or while they were caring for them.

The importance of dreams

The people of the longhouse believed that their dreams were very important and tried hard to figure out the meanings of the dreams. They also loved to guess one another's dreams and even help make them come true. They felt that if a dream did not come true, it might make someone ill. In the picture below, a man is shown dreaming about four masked men who are curing him of an illness. If his dream comes true, he will be cured. To make sure the man gets well, the women of his clan make masks like those in his dream. Four men then act out his dream so the sick man believes that he will be healed.

Change comes to the woodlands

Around 1600, the French and British came to North America, and over the next several years, they set up a large fur trade. Beaver fur was in great demand in Europe because it could be made into felt, which was used to make hats. The Europeans relied on Native people to hunt and trap the animals.

The Iroquoian nations traded furs for European items such as metal pots, knives, saws, fish hooks, and needles. They also traded for wheat flour, coffee, glass beads and woven cloth. As animals began to disappear from too much hunting, the Iroquoian people became more dependent on European goods for their livelihood. Eventually, they gave up rights to much of their land in return for food and supplies.

Europeans brought many new things that the Native people had not seen before, but they also brought diseases. Native people had never been exposed to the germs that caused diseases in Europe and had not developed an **immunity**, or resistance, to these germs. As they came into contact with more Europeans, they caught the diseases and passed them to one another. Many longhouse villages became empty when people died of diseases and others moved away to smaller villages.

Today, the descendants of people who lived in longhouses live in modern homes. Many, however, have revived the old traditions of their ancestors by gathering in brick or wooden longhouses to celebrate the rich culture of their past.

GLOSSARY

ancestor A person from whom another person is descended

band A group of Native people who live together in a village or camp

ceremonial lodge A small building that is used for celebrations, ceremonies, or special meetings

civil Relating to events that happen between groups of people in a village

clan A group of families related through a common ancestor

cornmeal Corn that has been pounded or ground for cooking

council A group of representatives who discuss and decide important matters

elder An older, respected member of a tribe or village

emblem A symbol, such as an animal, that visually represents a group

Five Nations A league made up of the Mohawk, Oneida, Onondaga, Cayuga, and Seneca Nations

girdle To cut bark away from a tree in a ring around the trunk

Haudenosaunee The name the Five Nations call themselves

hide The skin of an animal, which is cleaned, treated, and used to make clothing and other useful items

immunity The body's ability to resist disease or infection

indigenous Describing people or things that are native to an area

language group Several languages that are similar to one another because they share roots in a single language

lodge A dwelling place; a home

matron Clan mother and head of a clan

mortar and pestle A bowl and blunt instrument used together to grind foods such as corn or wheat into powder for cooking

rawhide Hide that has been dried, rather than tanned, to make it durable

regalia Items such as headdresses and belts that are worn in ceremonies

sachem The title of a male leader in a group; a chief

sinew The strong connective tissue of animals, which can be used as string or thread

Three Sisters The three essential crops of corn, beans, and squash; also the spirits of these crops

trench oven A ditch dug into the ground, heated with fire or hot rocks, and used for cooking large meals

tribe A group of people who share ancestors, beliefs, customs, and leaders

wampum Decorative strings of beads that often recorded stories; (A speaker held a wampum belt to show that he or she spoke the truth. A white wampum belt sent to another nation signified peace. A red belt meant war!)

INDEX

3 4 5 6 7 8 9 0 Printed in the U.S.A. 0 9 8 7 6 5 4 3 2